VOICES
BEHIND
THE
WALL

VOICES BEHIND THE WALL

NINETY PRISON STORIES

John P. Farrell

Henry Holt and Company   New York

Published by Henry Holt and Company, Inc.,
521 Fifth Avenue, New York, New York 10175.
Published simultaneously in Canada.

Library of Congress Cataloging in Publication Data
Farrell, John Patrick, 1939–
Voices behind the wall.
1. Prisons—Poetry   2. Prisoners—Poetry.
I. Title.
PS3556.A768V6   1986   811'.54   86–3019
ISBN: 0-8050-0052-6

First Edition

Printed in the United States of America
10 9 8 7 6 5 4 3 2 1

ISBN 0-8050-0052-6

DEDICATED TO

MY FATHER
and
to all prison inmates
who are sincerely trying
to change their lives
for the better

ACKNOWLEDGMENTS

This book is the result of the influence of many people. I am deeply grateful to the men who shared their stories, thoughts, and feelings with me; they made this book possible.

Many other people also contributed to this book in less obvious ways. Jane Allen and Bob Kirsch were more helpful than they realize. My wife, Jane, provided invaluable advice and emotional support. I am also grateful to my friend Terrence Winch for his encouragement and critical comments. My editor, Robert Cowley, made many useful suggestions, and my typist, Lucy Lather, deserves special mention.

VOICES BEHIND THE WALL

INTRODUCTION

Like Chaucer's pilgrims going to Canterbury, men in prison also have time to pass, and they often pass it by telling stories about their lives. Occasionally something important happens. People who are not accustomed to talking about themselves ventilate pain, inadvertently revealing their feelings to their comrades. Whenever a man can get some sort of emotional response to his story, he is for a moment less alone in the world, and these are all desperately lonely men.

During the years I have worked as a psychologist in a maximum-security prison on the East Coast, I have been collecting these stories. Some are from parolees, a few from guards or other prison employees, but the bulk of them have come from the inmates themselves. Originally I had no intention of publishing. I'd simply written down those comments that stuck in my mind, because I didn't want to forget them. After some years my desk drawers began to overfill with notebooks and scraps of paper. As a way of organizing these notes, I began to type out the most memorable of the tales. At first, quite without meaning to, I put them in a verse format; it seemed to fit. To preserve their freshness and immediacy, I retained the first-person-singular voice in which I heard them.

These stories illustrate a curious characteristic of prison inmates—a combination of strength and vulnerability that continues to surprise me even after years of working with them. Most are tough and dangerous men, but at the same time they are emotionally needy, dependent; their self-esteem is fragile, and they are extraordinarily sensitive to criticism and put-downs.

There is a similar paradox in their attitude toward women. They long for a perfect woman but can become angry and resentful of those who do not measure up. Those women who do not meet their expectations are considered something to be used or exploited. These feelings come out in several of the stories, particularly in "The Cow."

Oversentimentalizing these people may be a dangerous mistake. But one can try to understand them and why they turned to crime. As a prison psychologist, I've come to have some very definite feelings about crime and criminals, and many of the stories in this book bear out those feelings. For instance, it seems to me that the economic and environmental causes of crime have been overplayed. Certainly it is difficult for a child to grow up with fewer economic advantages, in an environment where he observes criminal behavior and where he sees drugs used regularly. But this is only a partial explanation for criminality. I have often seen prison guards and new inmates greet each other as a "home boy," meaning someone who grew up in the same neighborhood. I know guards and other prison employees, responsible men and good fathers, who grew up in the same inner-city housing projects as the people they watch over in prison. There are, moreover, prison inmates who grew up financially well-off in middle-class homes.

The vast majority of inmates with whom I have worked fit into two categories. One group had a chaotic early home life with little affection or nurturance. In the story "Pumpin' Ego," the man describes how the affection he missed contributed to his criminal behavior. The men who grew up in this kind of family also lacked a positive male role model. As a result they have inner doubts about their masculinity, which they camouflage by exaggerated bravado and macho behavior, like the man in "The Pistol" who needed a gun to feel more masculine. It is for this reason that the most inflammatory insults in a prison are "bitch," "punk," "faggot," and "whore"—all terms that impugn a man's masculinity.

The other group of criminals come from families with something of the opposite extreme, a type of over-indulgence that constantly ignores or excuses bad behavior. These men grew up thinking that nothing they did was their fault. It was always the other kid's fault, or if the child got into trouble at school, the teacher's fault. Children growing up with this kind of attitude never experience guilt or learn to respect the rights of others. The story "The Greatest Mother in the World" shows the effects of this kind of upbringing.

Regardless of a man's history, criminals are still responsible for their behavior. As long as a man blames his family, society, or other forces outside himself, he cannot be rehabilitated. I have never seen a successful rehabilitation take place until a man has first accepted responsibility for his life and then realizes that he has control over his future.

Another issue is the debate between those who advocate treatment and rehabilitative services versus those with a "law and order" approach advocating swift punishment, stiff sentences, and a three-time-loser law for repeat offenders. Both approaches are necessary. Rehabilitation is important because most of the men in prison eventually get out; obviously the less dangerous they are when they return to the street, the better. The particular institution where I collected these stories has a treatment program, but rehabilitation does not work unless it is backed up by stiff punishment. Effective rehabilitation programs must include intensive group psychotherapy to produce changes in personality and character. Surface insights or intellectual knowledge are not enough. The man who told the story "Staying Out" is a good example. He had decided that he would not return to crime and that he would stay out of prison, but his basic character and personality had not changed. His mocking of other inmates who did not share his intellectual conviction turned out to be ironic. After a short time on parole, he committed a serious crime and returned to prison with a sixty-year sentence.

Group therapy tends to be more effective with inmates than individual therapy: These men are superb con artists, but it is far more difficult for them to con each other than to con a middle-class therapist. For inmates, therapy involves facing intense inner pain, which they have been avoiding through various combinations of alcohol, drugs, and impulsive activities. Many of these men will go through this pain only because it makes parole more likely; they realize that the alternative is spending much of their lives behind bars.

A second reason for a combination of rehabilitation and stiff punishment is more basic. It is difficult for a man who once made six thousand dollars a week through, say, drug dealing and pimping or armed robberies, to settle for a hard and mundane job at two hundred a week. It is far easier for a man to avoid returning to the criminal life-style if he recognizes that it will lead to only a brief windfall, followed by years of incarceration.

Do treatment and rehabilitative services actually work, and are they worth the cost? My personal experience leads me to answer with a strong affirmative, but it is difficult to prove this statistically. We must compare the recidivism of inmates who went through treatment programs with that of similar inmates who did not receive treatment; unfortunately there are very few statistically sound studies on recidivism.

Even so, it is possible to make some generalizations. Murderers who knew their victim, for example—people who killed a spouse, lover, relative, or friend—tend to feel a great deal of remorse and *want* to change so that they will never again take a human life. This makes them good candidates for treatment programs. Armed robbers and burglars have potential for rehabilitation, but most of them have emotional problems as well as drug habits to overcome. Sexual criminals are the hardest to deal with. Men who have committed a number of rapes have a low success rate in treatment. These men have deep-seated pathologies that go beyond sex; many even have difficulty achieving erection when committing their crimes. They have usually committed far more rapes than they have been caught for, and although a few can be helped, many will rape again, even after treatment. Results with those who have committed crimes against children vary according to the type of crime. Parents who lose control and violently abuse their children have emotional problems and a lack of impulse control. These problems can be treated. On the other hand, men who sexually abuse children have low success rates in treatment. Like rapists, many repeat their crimes. In my view most judges are far too lenient in imposing sentence on both rapists and child molesters.

My purpose in this work is not to present a scientific treatise on crime or criminal behavior. But I hope that by using inmates' own words, I can give a glimpse into the criminal mind that ordinary people rarely encounter. Many have written about criminals—criminologists, psychologists, sociologists, government officials, journalists, and lawyers—everyone but the criminals themselves. Many of the expressions used in these stories are not familiar to the general reader, but the Glossary at the end of the book will help to explain them.

Of course all names have been changed to protect privacy, and details have been altered when a specific case might be identified. I have also avoided using identifiable details even when they were already a matter of public record. But every case has many similar counterparts, and no conclusions should be drawn regarding the identity of particular persons.

THE ANALYSIS OF THE SHRINK

You know that freaky shrink, Shapiro,
the one that thinks everything we say
is a sign we're really homosexuals,
an' he says the word *criminals*
like he's really pissed?

Shorty figures that when
Shapiro was a kid,
he got picked on an' beat up
by kids that was like us,
an' in that muthafucker's
subconscious mind,
he's still tryin' to get even.

ARCHIE

Archie told me
he's in here 'cause
he killed this guy
who tried to move in on him.
Archie talked about pimpin' these bitches,
catchin' planes, doin' drugs, and drivin' cars,
but I find out
he's in here for flashin'.
Can you imagine a guy
comin' to jail for somethin'
as dumb as flashin'?
Archie talked so big,
but he's just
a regular Flash Gordon.

ATTITUDE CHANGE

When I was nineteen I thought
my father was a chump.
He worked a job and a half,
givin' my mother his pay
and catchin' shit from her
if he went to the bar with his friends.
My buddies on the street use ta say,
"Man, you don't give money to a woman,
You get money from her."
My friends got me started
doin' Murphys, yokin',
and when I did my first robbery,
my heart was goin' a hundred miles an hour.
After a while I got use ta it,
and it wasn't no big thing.
Since I caught this charge
and came here,
I been talkin' ta older guys
and now I see my father was OK.
Most guys say they roll out
if their woman gets two or three kids.
My father stayed and took care of eight.
We always had food in our bellies,
a place to sleep, and clothes ta keep us warm.
My father was no chump,
he was standin' strong.

BAD THOUGHTS

I never knew
everybody gets bad thoughts.
I useta get bad thoughts
and I'd think,
"Damn, you a dirty muthafucker."
But now I know
everybody gets bad thoughts.
It's a spooky muthafucker.

BANGIN' 'SCRIPT

I forged prescriptions for Quaaludes.
I used them myself an' sold them at school,
but I wore out my welcome
at the drugstores where I lived,
so I went to this small town
about thirty miles out in the country
to bang 'script for 'ludes.
When I gave the 'script in this little drugstore,
they told me to come back in twenty minutes.
When I came back later
two guys in suits came out of the back.
I go for the door but one says, "Halt!"
an' he's got a pistol in his hand.
They put cuffs on me, bring me to jail,
an' throw me in a holdin' cell.
I was shocked.
I never saw anything like it—
people half naked, drunk, lyin' on the ground;
some had shit or pissed themselves.
They didn't give me a phone call for twelve hours,
then my brother came and bailed me out.
I felt really fucked up over that,
but not enough to stop dealin'.

THE BEAST

Every night or every two nights
I read these lust books
and masturbate.
After I'm done
I say I'm not
gonna do that again,
but the next night
or the night after,
I do it again.
Sometimes when I wipe that
cum off my stomach
and flush it down the toilet,
I wonder if I'm flushin' a soul
down the toilet.
I read in the Bible
that the Beast is gonna
come out of the sea.
Sometimes I worry that
my cum will go
through the sewer to the sea
and make the soul of the Beast.

THE BEST HUSTLE

Some guys wanna pimp a girl,
turn her out to work for them.
They get the girl on drugs
so she'll trick for her dope shots.
Other guys will get her high on booze and drugs,
fuck her, call some friends over to fuck her,
an' when she starts comin' down off the high,
they call her "whore" and "bitch."
She starts feelin' real low about herself
an' they got control,
she'll do what they want.
But those ways don't
give you the best hustle.
I pimped a lot of girls—
black, white, Chicano, and Vietnamese—
and I'll tell you
the best girls I ever had were AC/DC.
They'll make it with guys
earnin' you money,
and they'll make it with girls
they'll recruit for you.
A girl that's AC/DC
gives you the best hustle.

BIKER'S LAWYER

My lawyer got time for attempted bribery
when I got my conviction.
He kinda pissed me off because
I think I mighta had a shot
at beatin' my charge
with a straight defense,
but he was fucked up.
He had to do things illegal,
like he could've afforded to buy
all kinds of TVs from a store
but he wouldn't
if he could get one hot.
He liked to wear biker colors,
spend nights at our clubhouse,
an' fuck the whores an' sluts
that hung around there
instead of goin' home to his wife.
He had this nice brick house
in the suburbs, an' his wife
was fuckin' beautiful.
I talked to her once
when I brought some tires an' a stereo
over to pay my bill
an' she was really fuckin' beautiful.
I couldn't understand his fascination with us.
If I could've traded what I had
for what he had,
I'd do it in a minute.

BREAKING AND ENTERING

When I'd feel very depressed,
low and fucked up,
I'd know it was time
to do a burglary.
That feelin' that nuthin'
was goin' right and
that I was a failure
would change when
I got in one of those houses.
Then I'd be really alert,
feelin' very energetic and strong,
more than just on top of things,
it was almost like a high.
But when I'd drive away
I'd start comin' down
and begin to feel sick.
Then I'd pull over to the side
of the road
and vomit for fifteen minutes.

THE BRIDGE

This night I saw a girl get out of her car
an' walk toward her house.
I grabbed her from behind,
put my hand over her mouth
an' said, "Don't scream or I'll hurt you."
I dragged her into the woods
an' made her take her clothes off,
but I started to lose my erection
so I made her suck my dick
then I fucked her.
Afterwards I'm gettin' ready to leave
an' wonderin' what to do to her,
an' she says, "Wait a minute,
I'd like some more of that. Can I see you again?"
I told her meet me Sunday night
at eight o'clock in the park
by the wooden bridge.
I got high late Sunday afternoon,
go to the park to meet her
and when I get to the bridge,
six cop cars pull up
with me right in the middle.

CABIN FEVER

I'm readin' in the paper,
with all the snow we got this winter,
people got to stay in their houses
an' they're gettin' cabin fever.
Man, if them muthafuckers
wanna know about cabin fever
have 'em talk to me.
That time I was in seclusion
I saw a man sittin' on my toilet
who wasn't there.
I'd go to sleep
an' I'd dream about dogs
tellin' me to fuck them
or suck their dicks,
an' when I'm awake
my cell feels like
it's closin' in on me.
That's fuckin' cabin fever, man.

CHANGIN'

The math teacher helped me get my G.E.D.
an' we got friendly,
talkin' about basketball an' shit.
The guys asked me,
"How come you're gettin' friends with a roller?"
You start participatin' in therapy or counselin',
the guys ask, "You kissin' ass?"
You start takin' courses, readin',
not watchin' so much TV,
an' you're black, the guys ask
if you're a Tom.
When you start gettin' serious,
it bothers the guys who ain't serious,
an' guys that were your friends
will challenge you.
If you start changin',
you just got to lose some friends.

CHARLENE

I'm fuckin' this whore,
she's ten or fifteen years older than me,
but I'm home from the army
and I'm horny.
After I'm done
an' gettin' my clothes on,
she's lookin' at me
an' starts laughin'.
I ask her,
"What's so fuckin' funny?"
She says, "You're Marie's boy,
ain't you?"
I say, "Yeah, so what?"
She says, "I'm Charlene."
"Tell Marie you made it
with Charlene."
So I ask my mother,
"Who's Charlene?"
My mother's shocked.
She says no one in the family
talks about Charlene 'cause
she ran off—left years ago.
Charlene's her sister.

CHEEKY

These girls that come to the visitin' room
wearin' T-shirts with no bra
an' shorts so short
their cheeks are stickin' out,
don't they know a muthafucker
might be in here ten years?
You can look but
you better not touch.
One walked past me
when I was moppin' the floor
in the corridor to the visitin' room.
No guard was close enough to hear,
so I asked her,
"Can I have the panties,
just the panties?"
I'd steal some paprika from the kitchen,
sprinkle it on them,
an' I'd be happy
just sniffin'
an' eatin' them panties.

CHICKENS

This jail reminds me
of my family's farm.
If we had a chicken
with a sore on its back,
the other chickens would attack,
peck at that spot
'til that chicken had a bloody back.
That would fuck with me
an' sometimes I'd try
to beat them off
with a broom
'cause there'd be times
when I'd feel like that chicken.
Same thing happens here,
like that guy Moon Man.
He ain't wrapped too tight,
he's kinda crazy,
an' the other guys like
to fuck with him
an' set him off
instead of helpin' him.
I can't figure why
people do that
just like chickens.

CLOSE TO THE LINE

I saw drug addicts when I was a kid
comin' up in the black community.
I saw what they were doin'
to themselves and to our people,
and I hated them for that.
You'd see these guys at a party,
they'd shoot up, sit in a corner, and nod,
their head hangin' down,
slop drippin' out of their mouth.
I used some wine or reefer
if I wanted to get high;
I'd want to feel energetic,
move around, meet girls,
have a good time.
Some drug addicts will tell you
it's good for sex, you can't come,
so you can fuck like a super stud,
but that's bullshit.
You see drug addicts,
they're not even interested in pussy.
You see a drug addict shoot too much
or get some stuff that's too strong
and they overdose—
the others beat him to wake him up,
not to save him
but to find out where he got that good stuff
so they can get some too.
It's like they want to get
close as they can to that line
where you might live or die.

THE CLUB

I was a bouncer in this nightclub,
a customer would get half drunk
an' a whore would pick his pocket,
or the bartender would give him change
for a five when he paid with a twenty,
an' he'd get loud and make a scene.
If the other customers get upset
they leave, an' the money leaves,
so you want to get that muthafucker
outta there before he upsets the others.
You act sympathetic to him.
You listen to him an' say,
"Well, I'm tired of these muthafuckers
pullin' that shit. Let's get a cop."
Then he thinks you're on his side,
he goes out with you,
you pull him in the alley,
beat the shit outta him,
take any money he got left,
an' his watch an' ring too.
The cops are on the take,
so if he calls a cop,
he gets arrested—drunk and disorderly.
Only thing, I hit one guy too hard.
His head hit the pavement
an' he died on the street.
Now I'm in this joint.

COOL MAFIA GUYS:
A GUARD'S STORY

These Mafia guys
look so cool, but
when I worked with the state police
and we'd bust one
you wouldn't believe
the shit they'd have
in their bathrooms:
shit to go to sleep,
shit for acid stomach,
and all kinds of shit for nerves.
You talk to the guards
on the night shift
and they'll tell you:
These Mafia guys that look
so cool in the daytime,
they wake up at night
screamin'.

COUNTRY COUSIN

My cousin came up from the country
and lived with us when she went to school.
She was two years older than me,
pretty, but kind of quiet, and she didn't know anyone.
I showed her around, took her to parties,
tried to see she had a good time.
She starts comin' on to me,
takes my hand and puts it on her breast.
At first I backed off, but then I gave in,
an' we're screwin' a lot,
until one day I come home from school
and everyone is sittin' in the living room.
My father, my mother, my sisters, and
my cousin is sittin' there with her eyes all red.
My father starts yellin' at me, cursin' me,
then my aunt comes in, yellin' too.
She says, "You're not my nephew!"
I scream back, "Fuck you! You're not my aunt."
I went out the door and ran away.
While I was livin' on the road
I picked up this B and E charge
and got locked up.
Now when my mother and father come to visit
and bring family pictures,
I pretend not to look real close
at the ones with my cousin in them.
I say, "Oh, that's nice," and pass them on,
but I really try to see her,
how she looks and how she's doin'.
It's just that I'm embarrassed to show them
how much I care about her.

THE COW

The other night I had this dream,
I'm in this roomin' house
in bed with a cow, fuckin' it.
People are out in the hall,
an' the cow starts moanin', "Mooo, Mooo . . . "
while I'm screwin' it,
so I tell it, "Shuss, be quiet."
I don't want the people in the hall to hear.
I start screwin' faster, gettin' more excited,
an' as I come,
that cow turns into my wife.

CRABS IN A BARREL

Most guys in here
is just like crabs in a barrel.
If one can't get out,
he don't want no one else to get out,
so they fight an' pull each other down.
That basketball court is a danger zone.
A guy makes an accidental foul,
the next thing you know
one is sayin', "Bitch!"
the other is sayin', "Muthafucker!"
an' one gets cut
or hit across the side of his head
with batteries in a sock.
I seen guys get killed
over changin' the TV.
You got to be on guard all the time.
Even them religious types are bad,
they'll kill you an' say
they're doin' it for God.
You can't trust the faggies either.
Take Go-Go: he's a girl,
but he's nasty;
he'll put an ice pick in you quick.
A lot of those guys scare me
'cause they don't really want to fight
but they'll stand there sayin',
"Okay muthafucker, you wanna get down?"
They don't know they're sellin' death.
You see a guy get shanked up,
they put a blanket over him,
coverin' his face,

an' send him home to his people in a box.
I'm scared o' goin' home that way.
I really don't wanna die in jail.

DEALIN' AND SELLIN'

I think my mother
was a prostitute.
All her friends were.
I asked her and she said no,
but I think she was,
and that fucks me up.
The shrink asked me how
I supported my own kids,
an' I told him dealin' drugs.
Then he asks me
could I see
I was doin' the same thing
as my mother.
Man, that's bullshit.
I can't believe that.
There's a difference.
A pussy wasn't meant
to be sold.

DEAR WARDEN

Dear Warden:
   I need vitamin C
   or I get constipated
   and have colds all winter.
   I got the money in my account
   despite the person
   managing my affairs outside
   who is screwing me
   through stupidity and stealing.
   The guards won't let me order vitamin C
   unless the doctor approves.
   He says the prison diet is adequate
   and doesn't believe in extra vitamin C.
   What does he know?
   He can hardly speak English.
   Now I'm getting colds
   and I'm so constipated
   I have to insert my finger
   and dig it out.
   This is anything but pleasant,
   which I'm sure you can appreciate,
   so I am writing to
   request your help
   in this matter.
   Sincerely.

DEFINITION OF A MAN

If you're twenty-five
an' some older guy speaks to you,
talks to you like you're another man,
an' you're surprised,
it feels strange
he didn't speak to you
like you were a creep or somethin',
that's a shame.
It tells you
that you've been fucked over,
that someone's taught you
you don't meet
the definition of a man.

DENIAL

This guy called me a punk,
said I was takin' dick,
so I banged him in the mouth.
I ain't no homosexual.
I ain't one of them
muthafuckin' faggots.
Sure, I have sex with men,
but I'm the pitcher
not the catcher.

THE DOBERMAN

I always brought Big Al with me
when I made a buy dealin' coke.
Al's half crazy but he's really good
if there's a fight or a deal goes bad.
I got my coke from a guy who lived on the water.
Boats would bring it up to his place
and he'd let me know when I should
come over to buy a kilo.
Once we go over to his place and he's got this fierce Doberman,
it's growlin', lookin' like he'd tear you up,
but the guy tells him, "Down!"
and the dog lies down.
The guy goes out of the room,
Al reaches down, pats the dog,
and starts playin' with the dog's dick.
Al stops each time the guy comes back,
but Al finally jerks off the dog.
The guy doesn't know it;
we finish the deal and leave.
A couple of months later
we go back to make another buy,
but the dog's not there.
I ask the guy what happened to him,
and he says, "I had to sell
that goddamned dog.
I pay seventeen hundred dollars
to have him trained to guard this place,
attack when I told him,
but he was no fuckin' good.
Every time a stranger came here
he'd just roll over on his back,
all four feet stickin' up in the air."

THE DREAM

There was a lot of heroin in our neighborhood.
Both my mother and my aunt died from overdoses,
and my grandmother raised us.
All the guys I knew fired drugs,
and when I was sixteen they got me to try it.
At home the next day
my grandmother made me and my two cousins
strip down to our underwear.
She checked us over,
our arms, our armpits, the back of our legs.
I asked her what's she doin'.
She said, "Lookin' for needle marks.
Last night I had this dream,
someone was takin' stuff in a needle.
I had that dream before,
just before your mother and your aunt died.
That time I saw their faces in the dream,
this time I didn't, but I know it was someone in the family."
She checked us over for a long time
and she didn't find my needle mark,
but her dream scared me so much
I never fired drugs again.

DRESSIN' GOOD IS IMPORTANT

Dressin' good is important.
Like you're goin' out ta do
some armed robberies,
you wanna wear two sets of clothes,
stuff that's larger outside.
You throw it away later,
then if you get stopped, you say,
"That wasn't me.
I was jus' walkin' down the street."
You wanna wear good clothes underneath
in case you get jammed.
You don't wanna go ta jail
wearin' tennis shoes an' an old pea coat.
You wanna look good
so when you go in they say,
"Yeah, he's slick. He's cool."

DRUG ADDICT

Comin' up in my neighborhood,
the kids would dare you
to jump off the garage,
but I'd always be scared to jump.
Other guys would get in a big tire
and roll down the hill,
but I was afraid that tire
might go in the muthafuckin' street,
so they used to tease me
and call me a chump.
My lunch money used to get taken
by the slick guys on the street,
and I even kept a shirt at school
'cause sometimes they'd take my shirt.
I couldn't deal with that shit
but I was scared to fight.
As we got older some kid would
get pills or a joint of reefer
and some of them would be scared.
Then I could act tough and say,
"Yeah, give me one.
I'll smoke a muthafucker."
When I started usin' heroin,
I felt even better.
The slick guys know you're a drug addict,
they don't fuck with you 'cause they think
a drug addict's a treacherous muthafucker
who'll change up on you just like that.
I started doin' stickups for money
and I have a nice suit,
four or five hundred dollars,

and a pistol in my pocket.
Instead of bein' scared around people,
I'd be flamboyant.
But after a while
those drugs start to fuck you up
and you don't think too tough.
Once I was walkin' down Main Avenue
in broad daylight with a crowbar in my hand
to break in cars to get money for drugs.
Another time I woke up in the hospital
after I overdosed
and I had tubes goin' into my body
everywhere one could go,
even one up my dick.
When I got to this jail,
I had three teeth in my mouth
and I was down to a hundred thirty pounds.
That's what fuckin' drugs can do to you.

EMPATHY

The guys catch big rats on the loading dock
when they work bringin' in food.
They caught this rat,
put it in a big jar,
and showed it to me.
When I looked at it,
I saw it was pregnant
and it looked back at me,
right into my eyes.
I said to the guys,
"Hey, man, that's disgustin'.
If you're gonna kill it,
just kill it,
or else let it go.
But don't keep it in a jar."
I been here seven years
and this bit is really kickin' my ass,
so I don't like seein' this rat locked up,
especially it bein' pregnant and all.

ESCAPE

They caught that guy, Blaze,
tryin' to get over the wall last night.
I hear he's been in here three years
an' he got a letter from his wife
sayin' she's pregnant.
I did two years in the Camp Center
before I picked up this charge
an' came here.
That was minimum security,
an' a lot of guys would go on escape
or not come back from leaves,
an' it was always like Blaze,
family trouble, girl trouble,
or they'd get frustrated.
Christmastime, birthdays, an' anniversaries
are the worst.
What fucks me up though
is it's always the white guys
who go on escape.
I think black guys can handle jail
better than white guys.

THE EXAMPLE

When a buddy came over for a few drinks
and his wife called for him to come home,
I never let him hear the end of it.
I thought the man should run the house.
I dominated my wife,
and I terrorized her when I got drunk.
I'd break up shit,
shoot holes in the walls or ceiling,
and beat her.
Sometimes she'd call the police,
but later I'd always be able
to sweet talk her out of pressin' charges.
It was only when
the state's attorney put me on permanent stet
that I finally stopped.
Now my daughter's grown up
and she married a guy
who does the same thing to her.
When I first heard about it,
I wanted to kick his ass so bad
I thought about escape,
but when she visits me
and I tell her to press charges
or leave him, she just gets quiet
and doesn't come back
to visit me for a long time.
It really tears me up,
the price she's payin'
for my bad example.

EYE CONTACT

I didn't wanna go in that bar,
I was a stranger around there,
but my friend needed a drink.
We go in and right off
I see it's not my kind of place—
it's a younger crowd
and there's drunks and drag queens in there.
We order our drinks
and this guy is lookin' at me.
We make eye contact and he keeps starin'.
Maybe he was lookin' cause I'm wearing that
"don't nobody fuck with me tonight" face,
or maybe he just wanted to ask me
do I smoke that shit
or do I want to buy some ass,
but I'm feelin' paranoid,
and I had that muthafuckin' pistol.
He gets up and goes in the men's room.
I follow him in,
smack him across the head with the pistol,
and he starts goin' down.
I put a headlock on him,
ask him, "What the fuck are you lookin' at me for?"
Then I drag him into a stall
and beat him some more with that pistol.
Now I'm tryin' to learn
not to make things bigger than they are,
and walk away instead of feedin' to shit,
but I still feel paranoid
when a muthafucker stares at me.

FAILURE AND SUCCESS

Twice I started businesses—
auto repair and landscapin'—
and each time one got goin' good,
I fucked them up.
I had to sell everythin'.
When I had good clothes from head to toe,
and a wallet full of money,
I'd start to feel jumpy,
like something was wrong,
but I couldn't put my finger on it.
Then I'd start drinkin', gamblin',
get into fights,
and pick up these assault charges.
Funny thing, each time
one of those businesses failed,
I felt bad, sure,
but I felt relieved too,
like things were finally workin' out
the way they're supposed to.

FALSE DIP

I'm in Gino's buyin' chicken.
I'm waitin' for my chicken
an' this dude with this girl
gets in line behind me.
She's in back;
the dude don't see
she's lookin' at me,
givin' me da eye an' comin' on.
That fucks me up
'cause I don't want no beef
with this dude,
so I yells at her,
"What da fuck you lookin' at?"
The dude gets fucked up,
an' he makes a false dip,
puts his hand in his jacket
like he's got a pistol,
so I take out my pistol
an' shoot him.

FAMILIES

You think about families
and you think your family is OK.
You don't let a muthafucker
say somethin' about your family.
You love your sister and brother
because they're your sister and brother.
But my sister's got this little boy,
he's five or six,
and Sunday she brings him to the visitin' room.
She looks at him, laughs, and says,
"He can roll a joint o' reefer."
That ain't good for him,
and when I think about it
I got to say,
"Damn, my family's fucked up."

FAMILY PATTERN

First time I met my cousin
was in jail.
He was doin' twelve years
an' he had to do all twelve—
no parole. He was tough;
he always carried two knives,
one hidden in each shirt sleeve.
Two weeks after he got out
he tried to stick up
the same store where
I caught my charge.
He got shot
and he died
in that store.

FATHER

The neighbors were afraid o' my father.
He didn't back down the driveway,
he screeched down,
missin', goin' over curbs.
Once he was shoutin'
an' my mother said,
"Be quiet, the neighbors will hear."
He yelled, "Well, I'll give 'em
somethin' to hear!"
He grabbed his shotgun, went outside,
an' ran around the house,
firin' in the air.
Sober, he was nice,
kinda quiet an' shy.
Drunk, he beat us.
When I was seven or eight,
an' he came in drunk,
I useta think
someone tied up my real father
an' sent this muthafucker
back in his place.
Now he ain't drinkin'.
He's got cirrhosis o' the liver
an' he wakes up at night
talkin' to people who ain't there.
He's fallin' out, layin' on the floor,
pissin' himself.
Last week was the first time
he visited me in jail.
My mother says he wasn't comin'
'cause he don't like jails.

He said he came this time
'cause he don't think
he's gonna be around
to see me much longer.

THE FRUITY BAR

Me an' my rat buddy,
we were on our way
to do some burglaries
an' we stopped at this bar
for some whiskey to get keyed up
an' over that scared feelin',
but the bar turned out to be
the fruitiest bar I ever been in.
First, I went to the men's room
an' there was this coin machine,
so I started goin' at it with tools
from my jacket to get the money.
The bartender yells from the front,
"Hey, what're ya doin'?"
So I yelled,
"This machine took my quarter,"
an' he said, "Well,
I'll give you a quarter.
Don't wreck it."
Then we started drinkin'.
I hadn't known the bar was fruity,
but that was kinda erotic.
It started stimulatin' me
an' that surprised me.
This blond guy starts talkin' to me
an' buys me a drink.
After a while he says,
"Let's go over to my place."
I tell my rat buddy,
"Take off. I'm gonna go home
with this guy an' roll him."
So I went to his place.

I was a little drunk
an' started feelin' sorry for him
so we had sex, but
afterwards I felt dirty and ashamed
an' I started hittin' him.
I really fucked him up,
but ya know, I think
he knew he was gonna
get fucked up from Jump Street,
like it was a price
he had to pay
for bein' gay.

THE GAME

This girl worked for me trickin',
but we made our best money in this game:
She'd pick up a guy in a bar
an' bring him over to the house,
I'd sneak into the room,
take the wallet from his pants,
an' go back to the front door.
I'd bang it open
an' start yellin'.
She'd tell the guy,
"You better get out of here,
that's my husband."
He'd grab his pants an' run.
None ever came back for his wallet,
but once this guy didn't run.
He started fightin',
throwin' things at me,
an' I had to stab him.
He died,
they caught us.
She got five,
an' I got thirty.

GETTIN' RESPECT

I was the youngest,
four sisters, no brothers,
an' my father left before I was born.
When I was little
my sisters played with doll babies,
an' I didn't know any different
so I did that.
My sisters sat in front of the mirror
puttin' lipstick, powder, an' shit on,
an' I copied that too.
My mother saw me do it once
an' she smacked the shit outta me,
but I didn't understand why.
In school I got good grades,
sat up front near the teacher,
an' the other kids start callin' me
teacher's pet, sissy, an' faggot.
That really fucked with me,
an' when I got to be about fourteen
sometimes I even wondered
if I was gay myself.
Later I got this pistol
and I robbed some drug dealers,
that made me feel more like a man
an' it really helped with the guys.
You go around with a pistol rippin' dealers,
the cats get a whiff o' that shit,
they don't fuck with you.
They give you respect.

THE GOFER

I used to drink wine
an' smoke reefer with this guy, Slim,
that lived next to me.
I used to do things for him,
get what he wanted
and I was scared of him.
He was big
and he had really hurt some guys,
but things were excitin'
an' the girls came around
when he was there.
Sometimes for a joke
he'd call me names in front of them,
call me "cocksucker,"
an' everybody would laugh.
I'd laugh too, but inside
I was feelin' like a shit-ass.
I never said anything,
I just pawned that shit.
Then one day we were drinkin' wine,
we had a girl there
an' we were runnin' a train.
She said she'd take everybody but Slim,
an' he got pissed at me
'cause she was takin' me but not him.
He called me, "Bitch,"
so I called him, "Cocksucker!"
He came at me,
I stabbed him,
an' now I'm doin' twenty-five.

GOIN' NEAR DRUGS

If you even go near drugs
once you give them up,
it's like you done
woke up the muthafuckin' baby,
and it's gonna scream
'til you give it somethin',
and there's nuthin' else you can do.

THE GREATEST MOTHER
IN THE WORLD

If I want anythin', like a good radio,
I only got to ask my mother
an' I get it on the next visit.
It was always like that.
When I was a kid,
I wanted a motorbike or portable TV,
an' I didn't get it right off,
I only had to whine an' yell a little,
then I'd get it.
I was allowed to go anywhere,
stay out late as I wanted.
Sure, I was spoiled,
but I thought that my mother
was the greatest mother in the world.
After I grew up an' people said no
or I didn't get my way,
it really fucked with me.
I couldn't save for nuthin'.
If I wanted a car or somethin'
an' I didn't have the money,
I'd try to steal it.
I always thought that my mother
was the greatest mother in the world,
but now I wonder
if she even cared enough
to say no and then
put up with my bitchin'.

GUARDS

Some guards stand there
when you smoke pot,
some sell it to you,
and some bust you for it.
You wouldn't believe
some of the things
that happen in jail:
I seen male an' female guards fuckin',
I seen a female guard
suck an inmate's dick,
an' once in the upstate pen
I seen a male guard
suck an inmate's dick.
The guards scare me 'cause
a lot of 'em ain't
much fuckin' different from the inmates.
At five o'clock in the morning one guard
useta let Buck out of his cell
so he could fuck that homosexual Spicy
an' be back in time for mornin' chow.
You know Shorty,
he was a butcher in the kitchen,
an' the old warden useta tell him
he wanted some filet mignon.
Shorty would cut a bunch of it,
wrap it, label it dog food,
an' send it to the warden;
so the warden took care of Shorty.
Even though he had a life sentence,
him an' some other guys useta get passes
and go to that whorehouse

on the road toward town.
I'm OK with the guards;
I joke with 'em,
ask 'em how they're doin',
an' they like me.
I always got pot in my cell,
but when there's a shakedown,
it's like I'm the Immaculate Conception.
They come in my cell,
lift up the mattress,
drop it an' leave.
I never get busted,
but to tell you the truth,
to be fair an' do it right,
the best guards are the redneck ones
who's suspicious of everybody in jail.
They don't treat nobody special.

HANGIN' IT UP

You don't see us blacks
hangin' ourselves, takin' pills,
or cuttin' our wrists
like some of these white guys,
but that don't mean we don't do it.
When all this time I got
starts to kick my ass
and I really get the blues,
I think about settin' up a situation,
like a knife fight or a shoot-out
I know I couldn't win.

HANSEN'S WIFE

Hansen's wife sent him a tape
with her havin' sex with herself.
The mailroom guards checked that one
an' they were lissnin' to it
in the captain's office.
She's talkin' about what
she's doin' to herself,
makin' noises an' moanin'
for a half hour on the tape,
an' there was sweat
on the captain's forehead.
They couldn't understand it;
they were sayin'
she must be crazy
doin' somethin' like that,
but with Hansen
bein' in the joint with no pussy
for a couple of years,
I think what she tried to do for him
was kinda sweet.

HARRIET

Ads for bras and panties turned me on
when I was a teenager,
and when I got older
I came across this sex novel
about a gang of girls who captured a guy.
They forced him to have sex
and they put lipstick on him
and dressed him like a woman.
That book turned me on so much
I masturbated every time I read it.
I started wearing ladies stockings
and panties under my regular clothes,
and that would keep me excited all day.
In porno shops I found more books
and one had the address of a club
of guys like me.
I joined and went to meetings.
I learned how to use makeup
and alter dresses so they fit better.
Don't get me wrong, I'm not homosexual,
I only have sex with women.
The turn-on is hard to describe,
it's like I become a different person.
I'm Harry now,
but when I'm dressed,
I'm Harriet.
With makeup and a new dress
sometimes I get so excited
I'll get in the car and drive around all night,
even go without sleep for two days.
I've gotten into jams that way.
One night I was driving past an army base;

I had been so excited I never noticed
my gas was down to empty.
The car sputtered, I pulled off the highway
and stalled on the exit ramp.
It was raining; the guy in back
didn't see me in time and hit me.
He was an army courier
bringing secret papers to the base.
Because of his situation,
he had to call the MPs to investigate.
Two came—a big guy who wasn't bad
and a little wise-ass.
I'd been standing there in the rain,
checking the damage to my car
and giving them information.
My wig got soaked, my makeup was wet,
running down my face.
I wasn't Harriet anymore, I was Harry,
feeling embarrassed and really pissed.
Then the little wise-ass says to me,
"Jesus Christ, you don't need a car,
you need a goddamned broom!"
I grabbed him by the throat,
shoved him up against his patrol car,
and said, "Listen to me, you son of a bitch.
I've been standing in these high heels
for forty-five minutes and they hurt.
Get your information and then
get the fuck out of here!"
Just a short while after that
my company found out I was embezzling.

Sometimes I wonder if that little wise-ass
called my company and got them
to investigate me and caused me
to get this time.

THE HUSTLER

You know that guy they call New York —
he works in the auto shop an' he hustles?
When I first came here
he worked in the clothin' room,
an' my shoes wore out.
My feet were touchin' the floor
an' I was supposed to get state shoes,
but they could never find my size
'til I gave New York nine packs.
New York just went up to the parole board
an' he figured he'd make it.
He's got a lot of time in on his bit,
an' it's been a long time
since he got caught in trouble.
To have money when he got
back out there, he applied
for a loan from this loan company.
He wrote out the application
like he was a prison employee,
not an inmate.
The loan company found out,
bitched to the warden,
an' the board denied him parole.
New York out-hustled himself,
an' I'm happy as shit.

IMAGE

This ain't no pussy-assed jail.
You got to lift weights
an' be a macho man
just so somebody won't
stick a dick in you.
You got to be
a killer or a thriller,
and I don't want to be
a thriller—no punk boy —
so I act tough
and project the image
"You fuck with me
and I'll kick your ass."
But that ain't me.
I see someone help a kid on TV,
I get tears in my eyes,
an' I put a towel
over the window in my door
'cause I don't want no one to see
when I read my Bible.

INDEBTED

Gamblin' is a jailhouse thing;
there's gamblin' in every fuckin' jail,
but some guys don't let the stakes get too high.
They bullshit, tell jokes or stories when they play.
Other guys gamble hard.
Someone starts talkin', they say,
"Shut the fuck up and deal."
Squeaky, you know the guy who looks gay
only he says he ain't—
he's been playin' with Rocky,
and Rocky's a hard guy.
Squeaky's down eighty packs,
and that's deeper than he can pay.
Squeaky knows that with a guy like Rocky
if you can't pay,
you gonna get hurt
or you got to bend over.
I think Squeaky wanted to have sex with a man
from Jump Street and this is his way
of doin' it without admittin' he's gay.

JAIL SEX

Last night I started to jerk off,
fell asleep before I finished,
an' woke up this mornin'
with my drawers down around my knees.
Usin' your hand gets borin'
so a lot of guys in jail
use homosexuals or fuck boys.
Spicy is a homosexual
and Lenny is a fuck boy.
There's a difference.
One wants it, but the other
gets it taken.
Fuck boys are small, weak, an' easily influenced,
and they got resentment about bein' used.
You got to be careful around both
'cause sometimes they zap,
kill themselves or stab anyone.
The guys say the faggies go crazy
'cause they get cum drunk,
but I think they got to be
fucked up from Jump Street,
an' so many guys usin' them,
takin' advantage of their package—
that don't help them none.

JUMP STUDY

Some guys only piss in the sink
and hold their shit
'til they can use another toilet
'cause they're brewin' wine in theirs.
I like a joint once in a while
but I wouldn't touch the shit
some guys drink to get high.
They squeeze Old Spice stick deodorant
through a sock, drink the liquid
they wring out, and get sick.
Other guys drink rubbin' alcohol,
isopropyl. That'll fuck up your stomach,
but it's not as bad
as that fuckin' methanol.
That'll blind you.
Those guys just can't
get up off drinkin'.
They'll drink anythin'.
Not me.
When you dip your hand
in the toilet
and drink it to get high,
that's your fuckin' life
you're puttin' in your hand.

LIGHTS ON

I useta break in houses
only if there was lights on
an' I could see
people in there.
The other guys
broke in dark houses
they thought had nobody home,
but I was scared there might be
somebody in the dark
with a shotgun, and I figured
I was better off
knowin' where they was.
But when I think about it now,
I think I was on a suicide mission.

THE NICE GUY

Swamp Rat an' Touché were fightin'
in the dayroom,
an' Casey stopped it.
He's a new guard,
tryin' to be a nice guy,
an' he didn't write them up
for a violation.
He turned to us afterward
an' said, "Watch my back."
I felt like sayin',
"You better learn
to watch your own back, muthafucker."
If Swamp Rat an' Touché
get to fightin' again,
or one of them muthafuckers
gets hold of a shank
an' stabs the other,
the first fight is gonna come out,
an' it'll be Casey's ass.

NOT JAIL WISE

This is my first bit.
I wasn't jail wise
or schooled by no home boys.
I was shootin' T's
not knowin' how much,
an' I went out.
While I was out
I was assaulted.
Well, not assaulted,
I was sexually abused.
I'm no faggot,
so I'm embarrassed behind that.

THE OLD MAN KNEW

I asked Pop, the old man on our tier,
if I could borrow a small bottle.
He's a homosexual
but he knows a lot
an' he's OK.
He's got one on the table in his cell,
an' I ask if I can borrow it.
He says, "Why don't you
take the small plastic one instead?
It feels better in your ass
when you're jerkin' off."
It blew my mind
he said that.
How'd he know
that's why I wanted it?

THE PAPERBOY

This guy Buzz was a bully
in my neighborhood when I was a kid.
First time I met him, he came up to me and said,
"You're a punk."
I said, "Don't fuck with me," and he backed off.
I guess he respected me for standin' up to him,
but he used to pick on the weak guys.
Once three or four of us were playin' basketball
and the paperboy came through the neighborhood collectin'
    money.
Buzz says to us, "Let's get the paperboy
and take his money."
I said, "No, we don't hafta do that.
We all got money if you want an ice cream or a soda."
Buzz says, "No. A paperboy's a chump,
and you're supposed to take money from a chump
    muthafucker."
Buzz goes up to the paperboy and they start fightin'.
Buzz is a lot bigger
and we didn't go for what he was doin',
so we stayed out of it.
Buzz is hittin' the paperboy
and the paperboy's hittin' him back
with little short baby punches
to the stomach and chest.
We said, "Damn, if the paperboy's
gonna beat a guy like Buzz,
he's got to take a bigger swing."
Then Buzz stepped back,
and his eyes got real big.
We couldn't understand it:

He was only gettin' hit with baby punches.
Later we found the paperboy
had a little penknife in his hand.
Buzz fell to the ground and he died.
The paperboy got arrested, but they released him
on probation to the custody of his parents.
Buzz had a brother that wanted revenge.
He got three buddies and they came through the neighborhood
lookin' for the paperboy to fuck him up,
but they didn't find him. After about a week
they seemed to lose interest and stopped.
The paperboy kept deliverin' his papers.

PARANOID

I useta get these weird dreams
that scared the shit out of me,
so I took drugs to help me
stay awake an' not sleep.
Sometimes I'd get all pumped up on bam,
wide awake an' feelin' invincible,
or I'd fire cocaine, mainlinin' it,
over-ampin' so I didn't sleep for days.
Once I didn't sleep for seven days
an' it fucked me up.
I first realized somethin' was wrong
when I had trouble with my car.
I had the hood open,
an' this guy came over to help.
When he bent over to look in
I tried to stab him
in the back with my screwdriver,
but my brother grabbed my arm.
When we got it fixed
I drove out on the highway
an' I thought that the people in the other cars
were starin' at me,
so I really took off.
My brother said he better drive,
an' I got down on the floor
so they couldn't see me.
He took me home,
an' I started watchin' TV,
but I thought the guy tellin' the news
was watchin' me.
I turned the dial
to make the screen black,

but I could hear his voice
an' it still seemed like
he was talkin' to me,
so I went to the bedroom and locked myself in.
My mother an' father came over
an' my wife and them took me to the hospital
where they strapped me in this chair.
When my family went to leave
I got scared, pulled the straps off,
an' busted that chair up,
so my family let me go with them.
My wife started tellin' me it was OK
an' no one was tryin' to get me,
but that made me think
she was against me too,
so I smacked her in the mouth.
When they got me home
I locked myself in the bedroom again
for a few days, but it was weeks
before I was all right.
Cocaine, bam, an' not sleepin'
can really make you get paranoid.

PASTELS

My family sent me art supplies
that I got in my cell.
Sometimes I put pastels on my face:
blue over my eyes,
darken my eyebrows,
an' red on my lips.
Then I look at myself
in the mirror,
I start smilin'
an' jerk off.

THE PISTOL

If I started to leave the house
without my pistol, I felt strange,
like goin' out without my wallet,
an' I'd go back for it.
Usually I carried two pistols.
One was just a cheap throw-down,
somethin' I could toss on the ground
an' claim self-defense if I had to shoot someone:
I could say that was the other guy's,
he tried to shoot me first.
My pistol was a German officer's P-38.
I liked the power and heavy feel of it.
It had all matchin' numbers and a mint mark,
an' I kept it in perfect condition.
I carried it with me wherever I went:
It was next to me when I went to sleep
or when I was fuckin' my wife.
She was bisexual; she liked to have sex
with my buddy's wife
and she liked to screw him too.
They'd come over some nights
for a joint and a couple of drinks
an' we'd have a small sex party.
Both women got pregnant, an' to this day
I wonder if he's the father of my kid
or if I'm the father of his.
My wife liked those sex parties,
but deep down, I didn't.
It made me feel less than a man—
that I couldn't satisfy her by myself.
I guess carryin' that pistol

made me feel more masculine.

Besides, even though I couldn't rely on my wife, I could always rely on my pistol.

POINTS OF VIEW

This guy locked up his store
and came out carryin' a cloth money bag,
so I stuck him up.
I open the bag
and there's nothin' but mail in it,
then the cops pull up
and I'm caught.
I feel real stupid,
like I stuck up the mailman,
but Skins asks me,
"Would I feel better
if there was money in the bag?"
I say, "Sure,"
but Skins says,
"What's the difference
between rape and attempted rape?
Either way the woman still has the pussy
and a crime is a crime."

PROFITS

Last time I was out on parole
I started this paintin' business,
an' I was doin' OK,
makin' five or six hundred a week.
Then I had a chance to hustle some drugs
and make fifteen hundred in half an hour.
I looked at my paintin' stuff,
said, "Fuck this," an' started hustlin'.
At first I was doin' pretty good
but then I started havin' problems.
A few times I got ripped off.
Once I was makin' a deal on the second floor,
this guy grabbed the drugs,
jumped out the window, landed in the bushes,
an' ran off with both the drugs an' his money.
Other times I got stuck up
an' I got into some fire fights in parking lots.
I started carryin' both a shotgun
and a .44 that shot through cars.
It was makin' me get paranoid,
an' I got into coke myself, snortin' profits.
Now I think how hard I worked dealin',
goin' here, bein' there, the waitin',
bein' scared of both the police
an' gettin' ripped off,
I realize I would've had it easier
an' had more money at the end of the year
if I stayed paintin'.

PROVIN' YOURSELF

I wasn't circumcised when I was born.
All the other guys at school were,
and they used to look at me
in the shower or at the urinals.
Besides that, my older brother was gay.
My mother didn't know for a long time;
she got really upset when she found out,
an' then she starts checking on me.
I had the darkest hair in the family,
and once she looked at me funny,
asking if I was using mascara.
All that shit really bothered me,
especially since we didn't
have a father around.
It got so I wanted
to show them what I was about
when it came to sex.
With women, as soon as I could
get it up again after a climax,
I'd want to fuck again.
At first they would like it,
they'd think I was dynamite,
but after the second or third climax
they'd worry I was going to
get a heart attack.
I'd be laying there soaked in sweat,
trying to penetrate, talking out loud,
praying, asking God
to make it hard one more time
so I could fuck again.
Then the women would look at me kinda strange,
like they thought I was sick.
They'd avoid me after that.

PUMPIN' EGO

These guys hired me because I had the balls
and I could climb like a fuckin' cat
fifteen or twenty floors
up the side of a building
and break in an office
to get stocks and securities from a safe.
They paid me three thousand for a job,
while they got over a hundred thousand,
but they took care of me.
When I got arrested
my wife got a five-hundred-dollar check
every month I was in jail.
They'd tell me what a great job I was doin',
pumpin' up my ego,
makin' me feel I was important,
and that they cared about me.
My mother was a drunk,
my father left before I was born,
and I never had much of that feelin' before.
Sure, I knew those guys were usin' me,
but the way they made me feel,
I didn't even care about bein' used.
I just wanted to do
the best job I could for them.

RAT PARTNERS

I always did my burglaries alone
so I had control.
Only time I had a rat partner
it was fucked up.
He seemed OK at first,
but when we got inside that house
he went fuckin' crazy.
He went to their refrigerator,
stuffed food in his mouth,
drank their booze,
shit on the floor,
and pissed in the middle
of their bed.
I couldn't understand it.
I just wanted to get in there,
get money or somethin' to sell,
and get out again.
He was more interested
in fuckin' that place up
than takin' anythin'.
Rat partners just ain't reliable.

THE RESCUE

Buck asks me to act like a gorilla
an' bogart this new boy, Bunny,
so Buck can come over,
tell me to back off,
an' it'll look like
he's rescuin' Bunny.
Buck says if he's gonna
have sex with a man,
he's not gonna do it
with one o' them six-six weight lifters;
he's gonna do it with
a guy that looks like a girl.
Buck is givin' Bunny
reefer and cheese sandwiches
he steals from the kitchen.
Bunny is young, he's scared,
an' he don't know what's goin' on.
He looks real happy
when he thinks Buck is rescuin' him,
and he's smokin' that reefer
an' eatin' them cheese sandwiches.
Bunny doesn't realize there's a price
he's got to pay.
Buck is gonna tell him,
"Look, I took care of you
when you needed it,
now it's my turn. I need."
Buck is gonna scale that fish.

REVENGE

I go over to my girlfriend's house,
an' when I go through the bedroom,
the covers are pulled off
and there's a cum stain in the middle of the bed.
She said she was takin' a nap
and peed herself,
but I know a cum stain when I see it.
I wanted to hurt her,
but I'm on parole
and didn't wanna get pulled back in,
so I just turned around and left.
The next week she called me,
she cries, says she's really sorry
and asks me to forgive her.
I say, "Okay," we make a date,
and I take her dancin'.
We're on the way home afterwards,
we stop in a wooded area
to make out, and she gets real hot,
asks to go in the back seat.
She gets out the door,
but I don't climb over the seat,
I start the car and take off.
You wouldn't believe how good it felt
leavin' her there.

ROOT DOCTOR

My garage burned down.
My car an' motorcycle were in there,
but the insurance was fucked up
an' I didn't get much.
The same month I lost some money
an' I got hurt in an accident.
My girlfriend, Linda, tells me
all this shit is happenin'
'cause someone put this spell on me.
One night we're out dancin',
we run into one of her girlfriends,
an' she says she can see the spell, too.
Linda tells me she heard about
this root doctor with powers,
he can take away spells,
only he costs a lot.
I say OK
an' Linda sets up the meetin',
tells me bring eight hundred dollars,
an' we meet at night south o' town
in a clearin' on the river.
I get this funny feelin'
when Linda talks to the root doctor,
but I give him the money
an' he gives me this root to chew.
He draws this design
on the ground, lights these candles,
an' gives me a coconut.
He says stand with
my back to the river,
that he's gonna sing and when he stops,
throw the coconut over my head

into the river. After that
he tells me I'm OK,
the spell went with the coconut.
Next day at work
they get new machines
they wanna put in,
so they send us home early.
I go over to Linda's house.
This new car is out front,
but I don't think nuthin' of it.
I got a key an' I go in.
Linda is in bed with the root doctor,
an' I open up with my .38.
He's dead,
Linda is in the hospital,
an' I'm doin' thirty.

SEX OFFENSE, FIRST DEGREE

When I was fourteen this old guy
used to pay me to let him suck my dick.
It felt good and I liked the money,
but after a while it began to fuck with my head
and make me wonder if likin' it
meant that I was goin' gay.
I got real sensitive about
bein' called a faggot,
and later after I got married my wife found
she could really push my button callin' me that.
Once we were havin' dinner at my mother-in-law's;
my wife was mad at me for somethin'
and she called me a faggy
in front of the whole family.
I got so pissed I told her,
"When I get home I'm gonna beat your ass,"
then I got up and left.
While I was drivin' I saw this girl hitchhikin'.
I picked her up and asked her
if she wanted some marijuana.
We shared a joint
and she asked me to drive her to the mall,
but I took her to a wooded area,
I took out my knife
and told her to take off her clothes.
I wanted to fuck her
but I couldn't get hard
so I went down on her, ate her pussy.
Afterwards she asked me to take her to work
but I pushed her out of the car,
left her there, naked.
She called the cops, and since

I had threatened her with a deadly weapon
they made it, "sex offense, first degree,"
and that got me all this time.

SHAKIN'

I got this oil lamp;
it's against the rules
but I got it.
I'm readin' after lights out,
the guard comes by once
and he don't see it,
but I'm afraid he's gonna see
when he comes by again,
so I sprinkle water at the lamp,
but it's oil, see?
That oil splashes
and starts fires three or four
places in my cell.
I hit them out
with my blanket,
but some of that oil
falls on my sock
and burns my foot.
When ya burn yaself
somethin' cold feels good on it,
so I put my foot in the toilet.
I lay down half on my bunk
with my foot in the toilet
and I fall asleep.
I have this dream:
I'm in this field
with big grass and lots of bushes
and I'm runnin'
'cause this thing is chasin' me.
It's big and it don't have no head.
It starts catchin' me and

I fall rollin' over on my back.
I'm layin' there lookin' up
with this thing standin' over me
and it's got my shotgun,
the one I used to rob with.
I'm lookin' down the barrel
of my shotgun,
then I wake up
and I'm shakin'.

SLICK GUYS AND 'BAMAS

We laughed at the 'Bamas
when they walked past the corner
goin' to work carryin' their lunch
or comin' home smokin' their pipes.
We thought we were slick
'cause we got our money gamblin' and stickin' up.
We laughed at the 'Bamas,
but now we're locked up,
they're uptown,
an' they got our women.
When I get out I'm gonna get a job.
I don't wanna work in McDonald's
but if I got to work in McDonald's,
I'm gonna be a hamburger cookin' muthafucker.
Then I'm gonna get a corncob pipe
an' I'm gonna be a 'Bama.

THE SNITCH

Jo-Jo's a snitch.
He was my rat partner
an' he got caught two days
after we did some stickups;
somebody saw his license plate.
When I got picked up for questionin',
I knew he snitched,
an' when we were goin' to court
he turned state.
He's snitchin' here too,
so I take out carton contracts on him
an' once I set him up.
Currency is contraband
so I had two five-dollar bills put in his cell.
I figured they might think it was a set up
if only one was there,
but with two they'd think it belonged to him
'cause only one would be enough
for a set up.
It worked.
He got time in the hole.
I hear he's gay now.
I'd like to get twenty black guys
to line up and fuck him.
I wouldn't want twenty white guys
doin' it, 'cause he might like that.
Jo-Jo's a snitch
and a snitch
ain't nuthin' but a bitch.

SOME GUYS MAKE
YOU WONDER

Most guys are careful not to get caught,
but there's some guys I don't understand.
Take Frog: he drops his pistol
doin' a stickup.
Disco, he breaks in a house,
rapes the lady in her bed,
an' falls asleep after he comes.
She calls the cops
an' Disco wakes up
with a gun in his face.
Sky-Hook is another one:
He asks the lady for her money
after he rapes her,
she says she's only got a dollar,
can she write him a check?
Sky-Hook says OK an' tells her
his real name to put on the check.
Dusty, he acts like he gonna
buy somethin' at the liquor store,
an' they ask to see his license.
He forgets to take it back
when he pulls his pistol an' robs them.
These guys make you wonder
what the fuck they were tryin' to do.

SPEED

Before I picked up this charge
I was drivin' trucks
an' got strung out on speed.
One night I was haulin' this eighteen wheeler
across the Texas panhandle
an' I saw this giant.
His feet were bigger than my truck
an' he was stompin',
tryin' to squash me an' the truck.
First, I dodged him,
then I got the idea
I could kill him
if I shined my headlights
into his eyes.
He ran ahead of me,
I turned out my lights
so he couldn't see me,
an' when I came over the next rise,
he was runnin' toward me.
I pulled on the lights
an' got him in the eyes,
he threw his hands up over his face,
screamed, an' fell across the road.
When I crashed into his body
the hallucination broke
an' I was OK.
Next day I came back east
across that same stretch,
an' black skid marks
were all over
that muthafuckin' road.

SPIDER

Cigar, the guy in the next cell,
has got a jar where he keeps a big spider.
The other day he says,
"Hey man, look at this,"
passes me his jar, an' shows me
his spider eatin' a cockroach.
Man, I didn't wanna see that shit.
That night I was sittin' at my desk,
I felt somethin' brush my leg,
an' I jumped up on my bunk yellin'.
When I get back to my cell
at night after a movie,
I run to the back,
put on the light
an' look under the bunk.
It ain't just me.
Like in the movie hall Saturday night,
we were watchin' this horror flick,
a storm came up
an' we lost the lights.
You shoulda seen all these
scared muthafuckers jumpin',
holdin' on to each other,
when there was lightnin'.
It's like when I was on the street
an' robbed a store:
Inside I'd be scared,
almost ready to freeze,
but I acted like a super muthafucker.

STATUS LEVELS

You ever notice
how the rapists hang out together,
the murderers hang out together,
and so do the child molesters?
The murderers think
they're better than the rapists,
but the rapists say,
"At least I didn't kill no one."
The rapists are low,
but the child molesters are the lowest.
I useta do armed robberies
and I thought I wasn't as bad
as those other guys,
'til the last time I was out
and I got stuck up.
I found out gettin' a gun
stuck in your face
will take ten years off a muthafucker's life.
Now I don't think I'm so much
better than other guys.

STAYIN' OUT

Most guys in here
are assholes, drug addicts, or faggots.
They stand by the window
watchin' the front gate sayin',
"Muthafucker gettin' out.
Muthafucker gettin' out,"
but they don't talk about nuthin' but
who's got the best dope,
which basketball player's got
the biggest hands,
an' how to do stickups
without gettin' caught.
When them muthafuckers get out,
they won't stay on the street.
They'll be back.
When I get out
I ain't comin' back.

STEPFATHER

My father left before I was born,
an' when I was six
my mother married this guy Jimmy.
He worked hard an' was good to my mother,
but he was real quiet
an' didn't say much to us.
If I was fuckin' up he'd tell her,
"Your son is doin' this or that,"
and that fucked with me.
When I was a teenager
an' started gettin' into shit
I think I wanted him to say:
"You can't stay out that late,"
"I want you to stop gettin' high,"
or, "I'm tired o' findin' shit
that you stole from stores."
He never did that
an' I kept gettin' into deeper shit
'til I came here.
He's visitin' me now,
an' we're startin' to have some rap.
I'm comin' to see
I do good at my prison job
'cause I saw him work.
I treat my mother an' my girl with respect,
an' that's somethin' else I got from him.
Before I could only see
how he fucked up;
now I can see
he gave me more than I knew.

THREE HOTS AND A COT

The shrink asks me
if I like bein' in jail,
an' I ask him if
he's the one that's crazy.
He says I got it good here:
I hustle, run a little store,
sell sandwiches I steal from the kitchen,
buy a pint of whiskey from a guard for ten dollars
an' sell it to an inmate for twenty.
I sell reefer, keep enough for myself,
an' buy sex from punk boys.
The shrink says I got three hots an' a cot,
an' I don't have to
cook, pay rent, or make decisions.
They even tell me what clothes to wear.
The shrink reminds me
that last time I got out
I picked up this charge on work release
an' went back inside
before I even made parole.
I tell the shrink
that he's full o' shit, that jail sucks,
but to tell you the truth,
his question scares the shit outta me.

TWENTY-ONE

Monday was my birthday
an' when I went down
to do my job washin' pots,
Mrs. Jones, the civilian employee
who runs the kitchen,
brought out a birthday cake.
I just turned around and left.
I couldn't handle it, man.
I'm twenty-one years old
and I never had a birthday cake before.
I'd just figure
another muthafuckin' year went by.
Later I told her I'm sorry,
I'm not ungrateful,
I just couldn't handle it.

VIETNAM VET

There were two airfields where you could land
when they sent you to Vietnam.
We were supposed to fly into Da Nang, that's up north,
but when we got there they were shellin' the airfield.
Man, it looked like the Fourth of July down there.
We thought, "Oh shit, they're gonna wait
for the firing to stop, then swoop down
and bring us into that?"
But after an hour the firing didn't stop,
and they decided to fly us down south to Saigon.
We were all scared, and when we landed
we ran crouched down from the plane to the airport.
When they sent me to a unit out in the field
we got in some tough firefights,
and after one where we lost a lot of guys
I couldn't stop shakin'.
A buddy saw it, asked me
if I wanted something to take care of that,
and took out some heroin.
Back home I had smoked some reefer
and snorted both cocaine and heroin a few times,
but I never fired drugs before.
He showed me how to shoot up
and I felt better, it calmed me down.
After a while we didn't think much about home:
It was like we were on a different planet,
and if we talked about goin' home,
we said, "When we go back to the world."
At first I used drugs after combat,
but then I started bringin' them into the field.
I carried a set of works in my boot

and it helped you function.
If a buddy got killed,
it bothered you and you felt bad,
but when they put him in a bag and flew him out,
you didn't think about it.
There was a group of us usin' drugs,
and with that fear gone
we didn't mind volunteerin' for wild things.
Our company commander was amazed;
he thought we were a bunch of crazy muthafuckers.
After they sent us home I felt strange,
like I didn't fit in.
I was feelin' patriotic because of what we'd been through,
but I could see people weren't on that kind of time.
I didn't talk about it
but it fucked with me,
and I still had my habit.
At first I could handle it with my pay,
but it got too much: I did some stickups,
got jammed, and came here.
I've been off drugs for a while now
and I'm learnin' to handle things without them.

VIOLENCE AND DEATH

There were no Caucasians where I lived;
I never saw one
'til I went to school.
In school I liked to hit them
an' see that spot get red.
When I got older I started
takin' their lunch money,
breakin' in their lockers
an' stealin' their sneakers.
When I started to steal from stores
an' I'd get caught by the cops,
they'd be Caucasians;
so would the judge,
and the jail guards,
so I'd think they were fuckin' with me.
When I robbed this 7–11 store,
there was a guy in there
an' I use to steal his money at school.
He identified me,
came to court as a witness
when I got my fifteen years.
In court I'm sittin' there thinkin',
"Don't that muthafucker got nuthin'
better to do with his time than come here
an' testify against me?"
In prison I started stealin' their commissary,
an' if one was readin', it bothered me
'cause I didn't read too good.
I'd go up, take their book, an' say,
"What the fuck you readin'—
you think you're smart or somethin'?"
We raped this one guy,

he put street charges on us,
an' I got another ten years for sodomy.
Then the guys I hung out with started dyin'.
I was joggin' out in the yard
an' my best friend, Willy, came up the hill
zigzaggin', blood spurtin' out of his chest.
I stepped back so no guards would think I did it.
Willy fell on the ground,
he shook an' he died.
Another guy got his throat cut
an' one got cut across the stomach;
he was standin' there
with his guts in his hands.
Two guys got burned up
in their cell with a Molotov cocktail;
it smelled like meat,
an' they had to scrape them up
an' put them in plastic bags.
Most of that shit wasn't racial,
but all that violence and death
got me thinkin':
I can't keep livin' like this,
I got to change.
I got to do somethin' better.

VISITORS

Your visitors come down here talkin' about
how they're gettin' along with their old lady,
the way prices are goin' up on the street,
and needin' new brake shoes for their car—
things that don't mean nuttin' to you.
You're thinkin' about punk boys,
dealin' in coffee or cigarettes,
goin' to commissary,
gettin' high or gettin' over.
After you've been inside four or five years,
it's hard to even talk with your visitors.

WHEN YOU'RE IN JAIL

This guard is fucked up.
He's an asshole.
I told him,
"I don't like you,
you punk muthafucker,"
but then I think
now this guy's
gonna fuck with me
the rest of my time here,
so I swallow my pride.
I hate it
but I tell him
I had a bone up my ass
because my girl sent me a letter
an' I took it out on him.
I tell him I'm sorry.
When you're in jail
there's times
when you just got
to kiss ass.

WHY PATTERSON SOLD THE BAR

Denny, that little guy in the opposite cell,
I knew him on the street.
He hung out with this guy Bull,
a mean bastard who didn't take no shit
an' he really liked to kick ass.
A guy looks at Bull wrong,
Bull knocks his teeth out.
Bull gets pissed at a guy in a car with him,
Bull throws him out at sixty miles an hour.
Denny is little an' weak
but he wishes he could be like Bull,
so he gets real tight with Bull,
feedin' off him.
Sometimes Bull fucks over Denny too,
but Denny hangs in there.
Denny gets a good job, a union job—
Bull is takin' forty percent of his pay.
Once Bull put twenty-one stitches in his chin.
Another time Bull knocks him out,
leaves him lyin' in the street a half hour.
Denny's lucky he didn't get run over.
One day they're in Patterson's Bar,
Bull is drunk an' he's a mean drunk.
He starts beatin' on Denny,
calls him a pussy an' knocks him down.
Finally Denny bucks.
He gets up real slow an' says,
"If you're here when I get back,
I'm gonna kill ya."
Denny leaves, comes back an hour later
with a twelve-gauge.
He puts that shotgun four inches from Bull's head

and fires both barrels.
Blew Bull's head off,
blew his head all over the fuckin' wall.
Patterson's sittin' down at the end of his bar,
sees the whole thing.
They say he went crazy seein' that
an' he never got over it.
They say that's why he sold the bar.

WILDROOT

This cop, he asks me
if I turned fag
doin' so much time.
I told him why
I didn't turn fag.
If it started gettin' to me
I'd lock in,
take three or four hits of speed,
get my tube of Wildroot,
an' beat off for three hours.
I'll tell you, after that
you won't turn fag
but you can't
hardly walk.

WOMEN PROBLEMS

I got to be the manager of this fast-food place
an' these women my age,
they think a manager's got a lot of money.
Most of these women got a couple of kids,
they're alone an' havin' a tough time makin' it.
I don't look too bad,
an' they start comin' on to me.
I figure they're tryin' to use me,
so I'll reverse it an' use them.
I start collectin' phone numbers
an' pretty soon I'm fuckin'
every Susan, Jane, and Mary.
My wife never really knew,
but she suspected,
an' that didn't do my marriage any good.
At work, I'd have these papers to do
after closin' at ten;
that would take me to twelve,
then I'd have one woman waitin'
plus my wife to get home to.
If you wanna make it in the fast-food business,
you always got to be there checkin' on things,
so I had to get up early in the mornin'.
I used to get so tired,
once I was takin' a shit
an' I fell asleep on the toilet.
In here, without women, you wouldn't believe it,
but chasin' pussy, always thinkin' with your dick,
can get to be a drag.
Sometimes it gets to be another chore,
another thing in the day
you gotta get around to doin'.

YOUTH AND MATURITY

I get scared of these young guys,
these hoppers, eighteen, twenty years old.
They're not like the guys in jail
when I was that age.
In my day, you had a beef with a guy,
you'd say,
"Muthafucker, I'll kick your ass,"
and you'd fight him.
These young guys have a beef, they say,
"Muthafucker, I'll kill you,"
and they mean it.
They all carry ice picks or shanks.
Maybe they're scared.
When I was on the street
and I was in shape and feelin' good,
I didn't bother carryin' a knife or gun,
but when I was down or out of shape,
I felt I needed to be strapped down,
carryin' that pistol.
Guys that're insecure
are dangerous.

ZAP OUTS

The first day you go to jail
you got to learn:
You don't gamble,
you don't steal or fuck with nobody's drugs,
and you don't hang out with faggots
unless you want to get taken for a faggot.
The other thing you got to learn
is you don't take shit.
You take it,
everybody's gonna try to take your ass.
A guy says,
"Yeah, muthafucker, you ain't nuthin',"
you got to say,
"Man, get the fuck outta my face,"
or somethin' like that.
You feel better, too,
if you say somethin';
that shit don't stay on your mind
and you carry it around, maybe months.
But there's a few guys on zap time,
then you don't say nuthin'.
They ain't like other guys
you can argue with,
straighten thin's out.
A guy on zap time
don't care about goin' to the hole
or when he gets out.
He don't care about nuthin'.
A zap out says somethin',
you just got to carry that shit.

GLOSSARY OF PRISON SLANG

AC/DC—Bisexual.

bad bone—An untrue rumor.

bam—Preludin, or phenmetrazine hydrochloride. A stimulant that suppresses appetite and is used as a diet pill. As a drug of abuse, it is liquified and injected. Chronic abuse causes psychotic reactions and impotence in males.

'Bama—Literally, a person from Alabama, but used for a black man who is naïve or unsophisticated, particularly if he is from a rural area.

B and E—Breaking and entering.

bang—Depending on the context, this term can mean to punch, as in "I banged him in the mouth," or it can mean to submit forged material, as in "I went to the drugstore to bang this 'script."

bank—When a group of men beat up one person.

biker—A motorcycle rider, particularly if he belongs to a motorcycle gang.

bit—A prison sentence, e.g., "I have a ten-year bit."

bitch—Applied to a male, it is an accusation that he takes a female role in homosexuality. It is a highly provocative and dangerous insult.

bitch slap—To hit a man across the face with the open hand.

bogart—Used as a verb, it means to act tough, confrontational, and intimidating.

bone—Depending on the context, this word can mean a rumor or the penis.

boosting—Shoplifting.

buck—To resist.

burn—To swindle, particularly in drug deals.

carton contract—Having a man beaten up by paying another inmate a carton of cigarettes.

caught this charge—This figure of speech is used by most inmates when they refer to the crime for which they were convicted, regardless of whether or not they admit guilt.

cigarettes—Because money is forbidden in most prisons, cigarettes are an important item of exchange in the inmate economy.

coffee—Literally, instant coffee, another item of exchange.

contraband—Items forbidden to inmates.

cook—To mix a drug with water and heat it so that it can be injected.

crack, crack on—To put pressure on a man to submit to homosexual acts.

crank—Amphetamines.

crash—To become very sleepy or fall asleep, particularly after using alcohol or drugs.

creeping—Sneaking through office buildings stealing wallets, purses, etc.

dirtball—A person with a filthy cell and poor personal hygiene. Also referred to as a "crudball" or "scuzzball."

double habit—Dependent on two drugs simultaneously.

dummies—Phony drugs. This is a prison problem that often leads to violence when a person discovers that he has been swindled. Sometimes poisonous substances are also sold as drugs, e.g., any number of harmful white powders are often sold as heroin.

faggot, faggy—An inflammatory term when used as an insult.

fall out—To pass out or become unconscious without being hit, e.g., from alcohol, drugs, or an epileptic seizure.

false dip—To put one's hand into a pocket or inside a jacket, pretending to have a pistol.

feed off—To obtain vicarious satisfaction. For example, a man who does not have the courage to speak back to a guard might "feed off" another man who does.

feed to—To aggravate a situation, e.g., "I know he was mad and ready to fight, but I fed to it instead of trying to calm him down."

fire, fire drugs—To inject with a needle.

fish—A term, used for many years, for a new man in a prison.

flasher, Flash Gordon—An exhibitionist.

flat time—An entire sentence without parole.

fuck boy—A young man who takes a passive role in anal intercourse. Often these are weak men who are not homosexual by choice but have this role forced on them.

G.E.D.—Graduate Equivalency Diploma, a high-school-equivalency degree.

get down—Depending on the context, to engage in a violent fight or to participate in a sexual act.

getting in my face—Arguing or verbally challenging a man while standing very close to him.

getting over—Putting something over on others; manipulation or conning.

get up off drinking—To stop drinking. This term is usually used by men with alcohol problems, e.g., "I just can't get up off drinking."

girl—When applied to a man, an effeminate homosexual.

goon squad—A tactical squad of specially trained guards who deal with violence and disturbances in a prison.

gofer—A servile person who runs errands for others.

heart—Courage.

hole—A small, isolated cell where an inmate is put as punishment for violating prison rules.

home boy—Another inmate or even a prison employee who comes from the same area or neighborhood.

hopper—A young inmate, particularly if he is hyperactive.

hulk out—To expand the chest, raise the shoulders, etc., when angry or threatening.

jammed—Caught or arrested.

Jump Street—Initially, from the beginning, e.g., "I knew he was crazy from Jump Street."

jump study, jump steady—Wine made by inmates, usually brewed with fruit and sugar stolen from the prison kitchen.

kicking my bit—Horseplay, joking, or other behavior in a man that distracts himself from thinking about the length of his sentence.

lock in—To go into a cell and have the cell door locked.

mainline—To inject drugs directly into a vein.

Murphys, the Murphy game—A swindle in which a man pretends that he is a pimp and has a girl available but leaves after taking the customer's money. In cities this is usually done by going upstairs to the roof and crossing to another building.

over-amping—Injecting an excessive amount of drugs.

package—The image a person presents to the world: A combination of physical appearance, style, image, and personality. For example, "Because I'm small and quiet, he tried to take advantage of my package."

packs—Literally, packs of cigarettes, a principal means of exchange in the inmate economy.

P.C.—Protective custody.

physical therapy—Ironic expression denoting the use of excessive roughness in subduing an inmate or a criminal.

P's—Pyribenzamine, a prescription antihistamine; see *T's and P's*.

pump—To inject drugs with a syringe.

punk, punk boy—A male who takes a passive role in homosexual activities and is submissive. When used as an insult, the term is provocative and dangerous.

put a skirt on him—To force a man to submit sexually.

rabbit—To run or escape, e.g., "After he got that letter I knew he was gonna rabbit."

rat partner, rat buddy—A partner in crime or a codefendant.

roll—Depending on the context, to beat up a person and steal their money, or to leave or go. For example, "Let's roll," or "Let's roll out."

roller—One who leaves or goes, usually applied to guards or other prison employees because they can "roll out" at the end of each workday.

running a train—To engage in a form of group sex where one woman has sex with several men sequentially.

scale a fish—To take advantage of a new man in prison.

'script—Forged prescriptions.

selling me tickets—Using provoking or irritating behavior that might precipitate a fight.

shank—A homemade knife, originally made from the steel shank used as an arch support in shoes or boots.

shank up—To cut or stab a person with a homemade knife.

shooting gallery—A place where addicts congregate and inject drugs.

signify—To be nosy, prying or inquisitive, e.g., "He was over here signifying, but I didn't tell him anything."

slick legging—Sexual play with a girlfriend.

snitch—An informer.

spoon—Depending on context, it can be a tiny spoon used to serve cocaine, or a teaspoon made into a weapon by sharpening the handle to a point and wrapping the bowl portion with tape.

square business—Straightforward behavior.

stet—When a criminal charge is not pressed but the state has the option of prosecuting at a later time.

street charges—Charges filed with the state police or local police jurisdiction as opposed to infractions adjudicated by prison authorities.

taking it—Obtaining sex by force; rape.

tier—A section of a prison, similar to a ward of a hospital.

Tom—A subservient, unassertive black male. It is taken from Uncle Tom, a character in Harriet Beecher Stowe's novel, *Uncle Tom's Cabin*.

T's—Talwin, a prescription painkiller; see *T's and P's*.

T's and P's—Two drugs in pill form: Talwin, a painkiller, and Pyribenzamine, an antihistamine. The two pills are ground in combination, mixed with water, heated, and injected. This extremely dangerous process is said to give a high similar to heroin but at lower cost. Unfortunately, binders in the pills precipitate out and block the small blood vessels of the body, producing damage to the eyes, kidneys, lungs, and brain.

turn state—To provide state's evidence; to testify against a partner in crime in exchange for being charged with a lesser crime and possibly receiving a reduced sentence.

walking buddy—A close friend.

whore—Applied to a man, an accusation that he performs homosexual acts for pay. It is a dangerous insult.

yoking—A form of mugging or strong-arm robbery in which the victim is grabbed from behind with an arm around the throat.

zap out—To go crazy. Also, a crazy, unstable person.

zap time, to be on zap time—A certain period of time in which a person is crazy, or to be crazy.

3 8/90

Please Do Not Remove Card From Pocket

YOUR LIBRARY CARD

may be used at all library agencies. You
are, of course, responsible for all materials
checked out on it. As a courtesy to others
please return materials promptly. A service
charge is assessed for overdue materials.

The SAINT PAUL PUBLIC LIBRARY